CAREER STRATEGIES FOR

CHRISTIAN WOMEN

NEGOTIATE THE SALARY

YOU DESERVE

Career Strategies for Christian Women

Negotiate the Salary You Deserve

Leslie Knight

CAREER STRATEGIES FOR CHRISTIAN WOMEN
NEGOTIATE THE SALARY YOU DESERVE

©2015 Leslie Knight

Published by Leslie Knight

Cover design: Angie Zambrano https://www.fiverr.com/pro_ebookcovers

ISBN:9781515274759

First Published: 2015

For my nieces

*I wish you both every
success in your new careers.*

TABLE OF CONTENTS

*** The Notes to Self pages at the end of select chapters are short exercises for you to write down your thoughts as you are reading and thinking about negotiation.

ACKNOWLEDGMENTS

As with any book, it is rarely if ever, the effort of just one person. I was blessed along the way with the special insights and support of several people. I owe a debt of gratitude to:

Colleen Rudio, Tracy Allen and Bobbi Allen, three beautiful women who have encouraged and supported me. You've listened. You've shared your wisdom and best of all your wit. Thank you so much for the joy and laughter. I look forward to what the future holds for each of you.

Wendy Lipton-Dibner, friend, teacher, founder of The Action Movement and Move People to Action. You've had an amazing impact on my life. Thank you for your zeal, your guidance and your determination to make an impact on every life you touch. I enjoy our growing friendship.

Dr. Hal Dibner, another new friend. You helped me get through the barriers that were preventing this series from being written. You're very gifted and I'm grateful you are part of my life. Thank you.

Laura Steward, another new friend, author of *What Would a Wise Woman Do?* and radio show host of *It's All About the Questions*. Thank you for your encouragement and questions. They made a difference in a variety of ways.

Roberto Candelaria, another old friend. We've spent a lot of hours working with each other over the years. I'm so grateful for your support, the conversations and strategic insights. I look forward to the impact you will have on many, many people. Thank you.

Jeremiah Trnka, another old friend. We've walked through a lot. The best is yet to come. Thank you for your support and your faith in me.

Last but not least, my parents, Larry and Joan Knight. There's not enough ink to tell of all you have done for me or how you have influenced me. I am a Christian woman and leader because of your teaching and your example. Thank you so much for your faith in me and supporting me as I move into the next phase of my life.

Thank you very much! I have been greatly blessed by each one of you.

Negotiation is a learned skill.

Introduction

Just like any new college grad, I was excited to get my first real job offer. I said "yes" before the hiring manager finished speaking. I was so excited! My dream job! Wow! OK…I have to quit writing in my squeaky girly voice. I went to work in the IT Department of a large oil company. They hired my partner in crime, a black man, a week or two later. If I remember correctly, his starting salary was 10% higher.

Discrimination? Nah. The hiring manager was an older woman.

I had a few obstacles to overcome to reach my income potential: my Christian faith, my gender and my experiences. He started out making more money, but that's not the end of the story.

What is your income potential? Many of the factors impacting your salary are in your hands. Are you ready to make the money you feel you deserve? What will that get for you? How will your life be different?

I'll tell you a little secret: you can have the compensation you desire with a little hard work and effort. Competence and professional growth are required but they aren't the complete puzzle. I'm going to share with you the four missing pieces that will make all the difference for you.

1) Limiting beliefs and guiding rules (and what to do about them)

2) 10 things men know (that you should know)

3) How our patterns sabotage us in negotiation (and what to do about it)

4) A four-step process to win at the negotiation game

My goal is to give you enough information so you can successfully negotiate your first job offer, a raise or promotion.

You can be confident and have the compensation you desire and deserve. What will that get for you? Think about it for a moment. Let a picture form. Do you like that picture? Then it is time for you to take action.

Here's to your success!

*Change your thoughts and
you change your world.*

*~ Norman
Vincent Peale*

Rules & Limiting Beliefs

As Christians, we grew up with a few faith-based rules. Love God. Love your neighbor. Be kind. God will provide. Be content with what you have. If it is God's will. You can add many more to the list.

Rules protect us. They develop our faith and help us manage relationships.

Our faith is not the only source of rules. They also develop from our experiences. Each positive or negative experience creates rules so we can repeat or avoid results. They become a shortcut for our behaviors. When something happens, we don't think about it. We act based on our rules.

Unfortunately, they can become limiting beliefs that keep us stuck, just like an elephant tied to a stake with a rope. A shake of the leg would free him, but he is held in place because of the rules he learned.

What about you? Is there an invisible rule holding you back? Usually, we are not aware of its presence. They often reveal themselves in things we say aloud. Sometimes it is just the little voice in our heads.

Your thoughts matter. What does your little voice say when you think about negotiating a job offer, asking for a raise or promotion? Does it say:

- ❖ I'm not smart enough.

- ❖ I can't negotiate.

- ❖ I never win.

- ❖ That'll never happen.

- ❖ Be content with what you have.

Take a piece of paper and write down what you hear on the left side of the page. These beliefs indicate your rules. They may be positive or negative. Write them all down.

Now, on the right side of the page answer this question: what experience is associated with what the little voice said? Tell its story.

Is it your actual experience or the experience of someone you trust and respect? If it is someone else's experience, does it closely match your own? If not, you need to discount or even discard that data. They are reporting from their perspective. It is their story, not your story. If you are dealing with a negative belief, ask yourself, do I have an experience that disproves it? I bet you do.

One of my rules was "Don't toot your own horn." It almost kept me from getting my first real job. The other was "be content with what you have." If God had provided $xx,xxx and a specific position or a promotion didn't materialize, that was supposed to suffice. I was limiting my earning potential.

Faith based rules create special challenges. They can be difficult to put into perspective and harder to let go. They're often tied to Scriptures we have misapplied. In my case those were Romans 12:3, Proverbs 22:9 and 1 Timothy 6:8. I had to examine the Scriptures and the rules of the work place.

The truth is simple. Salary and position are how the work place keeps score. They are determined by your contributions and growth. Your superior doesn't see everything. It is up to you to tell them your accomplishments. If you don't, you won't receive the compensation your work merits.

The new rule was simple. It's OK to say what you did. When we talk about winning at negotiation, I will share a way to present your results that will get attention without feeling sleazy.

Pay attention to the little voice.

Examine the belief it expresses.

If it no longer serves you, replace it with a new rule.

I don't know your rules, but I know that if you don't let them go, your career is going to stall and you will never receive the compensation your talents deserve. How badly do you want that promotion and what it will allow you to have and do? Cross out your old rule and write down the new rule.

If you're looking for a couple of great books, I highly recommend *The 7 Habits of Highly Effective People* by Steven Covey. Beyond the Scriptures, it became my first resource for personal transformation.

The second book is more recent and equally good from a different perspective, *Shatter Your Speed Limits* by Wendy Lipton-Dibner. It is easy to see negotiation, your current salary or position as a speed limit problem and take action.

Eliminating those limiting beliefs will free you to win the game of negotiation.

Negotiate the Salary You Deserve

Notes to Self:

Write down the beliefs you hold about:
- Negotiation
- Your value
- Your ability to negotiate

Notes to Self:

Which of those beliefs no longer serve your best interest?

Negotiate the Salary You Deserve

Write down the new beliefs or rules.

*The objective of
every negotiation
is a win.*

What is your win?

What Men Know

Guys invented the negotiation game. Most men I know do very well at it. And yes, it is a game. Negotiation is a results-oriented event with winners and losers just like any other game. Seeing it as a game changes a man's perspective on the outcome.

Let's look at a car buying negotiation between men. They go back and forth haggling over price, options and financing, adding things in and taking things off the table. Voices may get loud and intense as they jockey for position. When they're done, they're both pretty satisfied and they shake hands. The salesman congratulates himself for getting a deal that meets his objectives. The buyer congratulates himself for paying less than he budgeted, getting more options or a great finance rate. Each thinks he won. Their perception of the transaction is all that matters. Sometimes they walk away without a deal. Rarely do they feel as if they lost.

Negotiate the Salary You Deserve

What do the guys know? Both men know that they have something the other man wants. The only question is whether they can work out an equitable trade. In working out the trade, they know:

1) This is a single transaction.

2) It isn't personal.

3) The objective is always a win.

4) Their win is clearly defined.

5) There are limits to what either of them is willing give up (a loss).

6) Asking for more doesn't jeopardize the transaction. It creates options.

7) If you don't ask, the answer is always "No."

8) "No" doesn't always mean "No."

9) Ask now, you won't get a second chance.

10) The game ends when someone walks away or both parties are satisfied.

If they have negotiated before or expect to do business again, they might alter their tactics a bit. However those ten things won't change.

A salary negotiation is similar to a car negotiation between two men (not what you see in commercials) without the intensity or combat.

Before the negotiation starts, the employer has a salary range determined by their budget. The low end of the range reflects less experience. The high end reflects greater experience. They can offer incentives to offset salary: bonus pay, stock options, cash in lieu of benefits (e.g. insurance coverage you don't need), time off and flexible work arrangements, etc. They can be very creative if you are willing to be creative too.

The employee's objective: get the best possible compensation package right now. He might not get a second chance. The employer's objective: spend as little as possible. Did you catch that? Let me repeat myself: The objective is to get the most for the least. It doesn't matter if the person on the other side of the table is a man or a woman. It doesn't matter if you're a man or a woman. Spend less is the goal.

Remember the negotiator's objective: Get the most you can while giving up the least.

Someone, preferably the employer, opens with a number. Then the back and forth begins. The employee will ask for the most that he wants and back down from there. Two or three rounds of offers will occur. Beyond that, the likelihood of someone leaving the table increases. Each has a clearly defined win in mind and they are not afraid to walk away.

As women, we tend to find the negotiation process distasteful. If you have paid much attention to car commercials over the last few years, you'll notice they use a no-hassle format to attract women buyers. They appeal to the relational nature of women and our aversion to negotiation. Unfortuately, salary negotiation doesn't work that way. If you don't negotiate, you leave money and benefits on the table.

How men and women handle negotiations has a lot to do with the hardwiring of our brains. It impacts how we see the world, interact with the world and the results we achieve.

Don't mentally walk away from the table before the negotiation begins.

Avoiding Self-Sabotage

At the heart of our differences is the lens through which we view the world. Men see relationships through the lens of results. In business, when a vendor fails to perform, men are comfortable firing the vendor after a couple of attempts to work things out. Women see results through the lens of relationships. She will usually do everything she can to keep the relationship though it might hurt her results. Men tend to focus on the result and the rules to achieve the result. Women tend to focus on the relationship. We have a hard time breaking up.

For women, negotiation tends to be about relationships, too. At times, that view serves us well. At other times, it can sabotage us. Our hardwiring makes the relationship feel more important than the result.

BRAIN HARDWIRING DIFFERENCES

If I were to summarize the key differences that impact negotiation, it would be these:

	FEMALE	MALE
Structure	Verbal Emotive Center	Spatial Mechanical Center
Structure	White matter	Gray matter
Neurohormone	Estrogen	Testosterone
Neurohormone	Oxytocin	

Our brains change throughout our lives. The structure and blood flow patterns are set during pregnancy. In girls, greater blood flow goes to the verbal-emotive centers on the left and right sides of the brain. In boys, greater blood flow goes to the verbal-emotive center on the left and the spatial-mechanical center on the right.

As you might guess, twice the processing power in the verbal-emotive centers will predispose us to experience our world through communication and emotion. In boys, the spatial-mechanical center along with testosterone predisposes them to experience their world physically.

If you give a little girl a doll, she will talk to it and make it a part of her relational games such as tea parties, house or school. She is practicing what she has seen in her significant relationships. Give that same doll to a little boy, he will most likely bend it, stretch it and bang it on the floor. He is learning, "what happens if…" and developing rules to govern what he learns that will later become systems.

White matter connects the left and right hemispheres of the brain as well as other structures. Women have more white matter. Combined with our larger hippocampus, the seat of memory, we have a greater ability to process more experiences and feelings quickly. The "look" that will stop a little girl in her tracks won't bother a little boy after the age of two or three. Her ability to process subtle facial and vocal cues starts as early as two years of age and the information follows us into adulthood.

White matter also allows us to assimilate and integrate information differently than men. As one woman described it, where men see one thing at a time, women see everything at once and the relationship between the pieces. We assess the state of a relationship through non-verbal and verbal cues as well as other pieces of information we have collected.

Men have more gray matter than women. Have you ever noticed a man intently focused on a project? Have you tried to interrupt him? That laser focus is gray matter processing in action. It also impacts how they assimilate information. They might not see the relationships between information that women do, but they are also not hampered by the extra information which often makes decisions easier.

Women also have a neurohormone coursing through their brains known as oxytocin, "the tend and befriend" hormone. Men have it too, but in a lesser amount. In women, this hormone surges during sex, childbirth, breastfeeding, skin to skin contact with our children and when we talk. It helps us to bond. It strengthens a relationship or it helps a relationship to start.

We also get a boost from dopamine. The more we talk, the more oxytocin is released. Our brain detects the pleasure of talking and bonding and releases dopamine as a reward. The more we bond, the better we feel, the more we talk. It's a crazy cycle. Our relationship building behavior is rewarded by the dopamine and we do it more. It feels physically good to us. You wonder why a teenage girl can't put her cell phone down. It's all about connection and relationship. Conversation is important to us…the deeper the better. It is about intimacy and friendship. We can pick up a strong relationship as though we were never apart because of the oxytocin, dopamine and the pleasant memories.

The male results orientation views conversation differently. It is about gathering information in order to achieve a result. For them, bonding happens during some physical activity, for example a ropes course or golf outing which is associated with a team achieving a result. To gather information, they simply need to be friendly, not necessarily friends with the other person. Oxytocin does not play a significant role in conversation for the men. For men, the negotiation conversation is just a transaction, a verbal form of "what happens if…"

Negotiate the Salary You Deserve

Men have more testosterone than women. Testosterone is responsible for risk taking behaviors. Negotiation is a risk. They might win. They might lose. However, if they don't engage, they definitely lose. It is always worth the risk.

Our Hardwiring & Negotiation

So, how does hardwiring impact our ability to negotiate? Let's begin with our view of relationship. We see the other person across the table or imagine them on the other end of the phone. We've been talking. Oxytocin and dopamine have had their impact. We automatically and unconsciously shift from friendly to friends. Friendship carries unconscious expectations such as we'll like each other and we'll do things for each other. It also exposes our fears…what if they don't like me? What if they think I'm asking too much? Am I asking too much?

We see something in their body language or hear something in their tone of voice that suggests discomfort and we automatically look to ourselves as the source and begin to question the reasonableness of our request. At that point, we have mentally walked away from the table. Our concern about a relationship will cause us to not ask, to ask for or accept less than what we want. We are more concerned about relationships and how we are perceived than compensation.

Here is how it happened to me. In entrepreneurial firms, relationships are often close as you share in the victories and setbacks of the business. I had access to more information than most. My superiors and I problem solved in casual conversation. A bond developed in me. Sometime later, every time I went to talk to my boss about a raise I would get derailed. He would tell me about the sad state of affairs and I would invariably walk away without asking. I could not broach the subject if I felt I would be contributing to his woes. I had a "relationship" and influence that I was not willing to risk.

Focus on the result. Your salary, your lifestyle and your perceived value are your responsibility.

White matter processing allowed me to see the relationship between my request and the potential impact on my co-workers, my employer and the list goes on. It really does not take much to derail the request. As women, we have a lot of information at our finger tips. Unconsciously, I was concerned that my request might hurt my influence. When we walk away from the table, we can find ourselves resenting the work and discounting our value. This is the beginning of a negative spiral from which recovering can be hard.

There is an upside. White matter processing will allow

us to see possibilities that a man might not see. For example, if you are told "we can't do _____" you can easily come up with possibilities to which they might be able to say yes. You might want greater flexibility in your hours to take care of elderly parents or a telecommuting arrangement. What will contribute to the lifestyle you want?

Lest I leave you thinking we're terrible negotiators, understand we're not. Anyone who can talk a child into eating their peas or taking their medicine has skills. We're concerned about results while maintaining the relationship. That perspective has a place in the business world. When it comes to your compensation, you need to focus on the result you want.

What to Do

Your ability to read facial cues and body language, combined with your ability to make connections between pieces of information is a formidable asset. On the other hand, the relationship drive can cause you to settle for less than what you want.

Blending the male and female perspectives will focus you on results rather than worrying about what the negotiator might be thinking. Remember:

❖ Your win is important. It is probably bigger than just the dollar amount and is connected to many things.

➢ Clearly define your win.

➢ Connect to it emotionally. What does it do for you?

➢ Ask for what you want; you might not get a second chance. It sounds selfish. It isn't and we'll talk about it later.

❖ Negotiations require give and take, not friendship. We can't stop the effect of oxytocin. We can't stop our natural empathy if we see discomfort in the negotiator. We can keep them from derailing the request. Ask what is making them uncomfortable. Use your ability to see connections and possibilities to create more options to get what is most important to you.

Tip:
Focus on the result.

Think friendly, not friends.

Remember, it isn't personal.

❖ Salary negotiation isn't personal. The negotiator's focus is on budget and policy. It feels personal because it represents your perception of your value and your dreams. Keep your emotions in check. We'll talk about how to deal with "No" shortly.

Superiors want to be generous and fair, yet sometimes they are limited. Proper preparation will improve your chances of getting what you want.

Define your win:
what you want
and
what you can live
without.

WINNING AT NEGOTIATION

Winning at the salary negotiation game is not hard. It's not like you're trying to negotiate the merger of two major airlines or Middle East peace. The process is pretty straightforward:

❖ Prepare

❖ Practice

❖ Present

❖ Part ways

The major differences tend to be in preparation, whether you are negotiating your first job offer, within your current company or with a new company as an experienced hire.

The Two Most Common Mistakes Women Make

I've already alluded to one of them. We leave money or benefits on the table simply because we don't ask. Preparation and practice remedy that mistake. The other mistake is a little less obvious. Answer this question: where do you want to be in terms of your lifestyle, career and salary two years from now? Five years from now? Be very clear.

Most young men I talk with have a clear picture of the career results they want, both financially and in terms of their role. Admittedly, when I began my career, I didn't have a clue what was possible. The Information Technology field was pretty new. My picture had more to do with lifestyle and a far off goal of having my own business someday.

The answer to the question about your career, salary and lifestyle impacts several things, including the size of the company for which you may want to work. Smaller companies may not have regular processes for raises or promotions. You will have to take charge of your career planning to ensure you reach your goals. On the upside, they often have the flexibility to do things a larger company wouldn't consider in terms of your lifestyle as well as provide interesting growth opportunities. Larger companies with HR departments and well defined processes will be able to work with you to provide planned growth opportunities. Management is rewarded for developing subordinates.

I have worked for large Fortune 50 companies and smaller entrepreneurial companies and enjoyed both. A piece of advice: if you want to own a business, you will be better served working for an entrepreneurial company earlier in your career rather than later. It's the only thing I would have done differently.

You are responsible for designing your career and lifestyle. You can live a life you design or the one you get by default. Which do you prefer?

~ Leslie

First Real Job Offer

As I shared earlier, I didn't think to ask for more. I was simply thrilled about the prospect of launching my career. If I had followed this process I might have had a different result or possibly no job. It's a risk.

You have an advantage that I did not have when I began my career: the internet. You can research anything quickly and easily. Take advantage of it!

Prepare

Do your homework.

❖ Know the salary range for an inexperienced new hire in that city, industry and role. Salary.com, PayScale.com, a headhunter, your school's career office or recruiter are different resources with access to the information.

❖ Google the company. What are people saying about it? What concerns you about working for this company? Health benefits? Process for raises and promotions? Savings plans? Their reputation?

❖ Are there incidental costs for the job (e.g. continuing education, licensing, materials)? If those costs are borne by you and not reimbursed by the company, then you need to account for them in your salary or budget.

❖ Know your numbers. How much salary do you need to live in that city? Appendix A has a list of typical expenses you can use for planning. Don't dig a financial hole for yourself if you say yes to a position.

❖ Know what you want in terms of cash, intangibles and lifestyle. This is an opportunity to create the lifestyle you want.

PRACTICE

Pretend you received an offer. Ask a friend or two to role play as a negotiator, preferably a man and a woman to get a balanced perspective. Give them the offer you want: salary, benefits, etc. Ask them to make you an offer. You respond. They counter.

During the role play, focus on two areas.

❖ Your emotions. Notice what is going on in your head while you role play. Make a counter offer. Get used to the feeling of asking for what you want. Get used to the feeling of hearing "no" in the form of their counter offer and regrouping. The more you practice, the more comfortable you will become.

❖ Your language. Avoid words like "concerned", "anxious", "probably", "maybe", "likely". They make you sound uncertain. A reasonably skilled negotiator will sense that and take it as a hint that you might be willing to accept less.

PRESENT

When they make the offer, ask for time to consider their offer. This tactic allows time for the emotion to dissipate so you can see things objectively. Should they make the offer at your initial interview, you definitely need to step back.

Celebrate! They have obviously chosen you above the other candidates.

Is your homework complete? Is there anything else you want or need? What are your concerns? Does the salary cover your projected expenses? If not, you need to make a counter offer. Do you need relocation assistance? Now is the time to ask. Have they answered all of your questions about benefits? Future raises and promotions?

Prepare your counter offer and present it. It should address your concerns and include:

❖ Your proposed salary figure.

❖ A request for allowances, such as relocation, parking, licensing, materials, etc.

❖ Anything you want to cover (future incremental increases, etc.)

They might say "no" to your salary proposal for any number of reasons, from budget to it being outside the pay grade for that job. They may be able to offer a signing bonus to make up the difference. Listen for what they are offering. Remember, "no" doesn't always mean "no". If this is your dream job ask if they are open to reviewing your performance and salary after six months to increase it closer to the number you want.

Part Ways

Sometimes the best option if they can't meet your requirements is to walk away. Don't be afraid to do so. True win-win negotiations, where all parties get everything they want, are very rare. The employer's mandate is to start low and sweeten the deal to get the employee for the lowest cost possible. You want to negotiate for your win, which requires starting high. Hopefully you'll get all of what you want. Usually, both parties give something up.

The question is, "are you giving up too much?" I can assure you, they won't. You don't want to take the offer and then resent doing the work. Life is far too short to resent the work, the employer or yourself for making a poor choice.

Don't settle for less than what you want. It's OK to walk away.

Negotiation is a process. It isn't rocket science. If you prepare well, you will succeed.

Negotiating Within Your Current Company

Time for a raise or promotion?

The process doesn't change. What you do within each step could change quite a bit.

Prepare. Prepare. Prepare!

I can't say it enough. Negotiation is about hard data, not feelings.

❖ Determine the salary range for the position outside of your company.

❖ Ask HR for the salary range for your current role and the role you seek. Their objective is to promote you before you get to the middle of your current salary range. Why? The middle of your current range is close to the low end of the range for the next position. If you pass the middle of your current range without a promotion, you have become unpromotable.

❖ List skills you've added or upgraded.

Tip:

❖ Clarify the value of the results you produced. How much did you save or make the company? If you automated a task that took 40 hours a month and now it takes 2 hours that is a tangible result in time and money. Tangible results could

Keep an annual IDidIt file to record your accomplishments.

See Appendix C for more information.

include projects completed on time or under budget, new clients or renewals and reducing errors and so on.

❖ Examine the intangibles. They have a measurable result too. For example, my supervisor recognized that my cubicle was the place the team gathered to solve problems. After looking at the data, I realized that most of those problems never recurred. If the cost for one occurrence was $50,000 and the problem persisted until we gathered in my office then I could quantify cost in terms of time and money. Ask the question: how did that help? Ask it three or four times. By peeling away the layers of the onion, you will get to a tangible result you can measure.

❖ State your results powerfully. We think about this when writing a resume but it is useful for a promotion or raise. The formula is simple: Accomplishment + Measurement + Means.

➢ Accomplishments begin with a verb: contributed, reduced, negotiated, increased, managed, etc.

➢ Measurement: how does this compare with the past or some other known data?

➢ Means: how did you do it? Here are some examples:

✓ Reduced monthly scheduled maintenance 75% from 64 to 16 hours through automation and process redesign

✓ Increased revenues from existing clients 50% from $150,000 to $225,000 by recommending additional consulting services

✓ Reduced recurring problems 100% compared to 25% the previous two years by implementing a post-mortem process

✓ Spearheaded effort to reduce recurring problems 100% saving the company $250,000 in one year by post-mortem process

❖ Define your win. What do you want in terms of your lifestyle? What do you want in terms of cash and intangibles such as flexibility in your hours, vacation time or telecommuting? What are you willing to exchange between cash and intangibles? What extra responsibilities are you willing to take on in return? They might be prepared to give you what you ask, but they will want something in return. It isn't just about rewarding your accomplishments. It's about what you are going to do for them in the future.

❖ Identify your manager's goals and objectives. How have your efforts helped to meet those goals? If you can present your case in terms of their objectives, what they really want for the department or company, your chances improve.

❖ Ask, "How does my competence and level of responsibility compare to the others?" Are you still being treated like the junior member? Or have you stepped up in ways that say you're as talented and competent as the senior members?

PRACTICE

You've already done this once, but if it has been a while, you might feel a bit rusty. Ask a friend to role play and focus on three things.

❖ Your language. Women tend to downplay their accomplishments. I can assure you the men don't. It is OK to say you were part of a team, but don't let that detract from your contribution. State your accomplishments powerfully as you did in preparation. Avoid "I feel." Your feelings are not relevant to the conversation.

❖ Your emotions. Ask them to turn you down so you feel the emotions and regroup. Be sure to role play with a man and with a woman to get a different perspective on your accomplishments. Verbalizing your thoughts will clarify your points. You'll be more confident, present your case more clearly and increase your chances for success.

❖ Your future. Often these conversations turn to projects and future opportunities and challenges. Avoid words like "might", "likely", "maybe", or "probably" when talking about solutions. They do not paint a confident picture. Be careful with "I think" as it can make you sound uncertain. If you have a solution to their challenges, state it with confidence.

Present

❖ Ask for an appointment and make your request. Don't blindside your boss. Give them a chance to prepare. Simply say, "I would like to talk to you about the possibility of a raise/promotion. When can I get on your calendar?"

❖ During the meeting, be professional, not emotional. If you are passionate, express it in terms of your results and meeting their objectives or passion for the company, not your feelings about why you deserve the raise or promotion.

➢ Avoid weak language: "I think", "probably", etc.

➢ Speak powerfully about your results. State them like you wrote them.

❖ If they say "No" in any form then ask follow-up questions. Avoid "why" as it is seen as a challenge. You might ask simply, "What stands in the way?" It might be a spending freeze. Ask when you can revisit the issue, put the date on your calendar and repeat the process.

❖ If your request is denied because of a performance issue, don't panic or become emotional. Sometimes all you need is a little time to change their perception.

➢ Ask what needs to change and how they would measure progress.

➢ Ask for their help in creating a plan to correct the issue. Their job is to develop their people.

➢ Track your progress.

➢ Ask for the opportunity to revisit your request.

❖ Remember, this is just a transaction. It isn't personal. I know that's a challenge. We are talking about our work or our value to our immediate superior. It is as much about our relationship to them as it is the money and we can see "No" as an indicator of a relationship problem. Most of them want to give promotions and increases. It is your job to make it easy for them to say "Yes" – so prepare!

Part Ways

NEW JOB?
☑ YES
☐ NO

Like the Kenny Rogers song says, "know when to walk away, know when to run." You might be working for someone who does not value you or your work.

You're in a win-lose situation. They are getting the benefits. You are not getting the reward. It's a painful realization. Be prepared to walk away.

I know. You're thinking better the devil you know than the one you don't. Wrong. If the role you are in no longer serves you, grows you, or brings you joy, it's time to change. Life is too short to be miserable two-thousand hours a year. Start looking for that new job and prepare your transition plan. Then resign.

You're probably thinking...but I can't resign. I have to _____ (fill in the blank). Listen to yourself. "I have to" suggests you have no choice. You're not in control of your destiny. Is that really true? Is someone holding a gun to your head telling you to work for that person in that company or else? I didn't think so.

It's scary. I know. I've done it. In the end, the change was far more rewarding. It will be for you, too.

If a role no longer serves you,
grows you or brings you joy, it's
time to change.
~ Leslie

NEGOTIATING WITH A NEW COMPANY

Sometimes that dream job turns into a nightmare and you find yourself looking for a new job pretty quickly. The upside is that you have experience. If you have been offered a job with a new company, the same steps apply:

❖ Prepare. Know:

➢ The salary range for your job description or job title.

➢ The value of the results you produced.

➢ The value of the results relative to the role they are seeking. You might have more skills than they are looking for and should be compensated for them.

➢ What you want in terms of compensation: cash and intangibles. Be clear about what you are willing to exchange and what is non-negotiable.

➢ The company's objectives and those of the person for whom you will be working.

❖ Practice. This step isn't any different from the others.

❖ Present. When they offer, ask for time to consider their offer then counter. You don't need to give them a reason behind your request just when to expect your response.

➢ Don't panic. You won't jeopardize your chances with a counter offer that meets your needs.

➢ They may come back with a different offer based on what they can do. If so, ask for time, but don't spend an inordinate amount of time considering the offer. You don't want to appear indecisive. If you can give them an answer immediately, go for it.

➢ Ask for all that you want in the first round. You might not get a second chance.

❖ Walk away if the offer doesn't feel right. What? Yes. I said feel and I said walk away. Ladies, we have an intuitive sense that we often ignore to our peril. The little voice may be telling you their offer isn't enough based on the effort you know will be required or it doesn't work for the lifestyle you want. You don't want to accept the offer and then resent the work and be looking for another job. Walk away and give yourself the chance to find the right position. Life is too short to be miserable in a job.

NOTES TO SELF:

Prepare - Define the lifestyle and career results you desire. Be specific. Use pictures if needed. The more concrete you are the easier it is for you to connect to your dream. Save this page or create a page in your journal.

NEGOTIATE THE SALARY YOU DESERVE

NOTES TO SELF:

Prepare - Determine the amount of cash you require for that lifestyle. Determine the intangibles as well.

NOTES TO SELF:

Prepare - Begin thinking about the steps you need to take to achieve the results you want in your career. Write it down.

Negotiate the Salary You Deserve

Notes to Self:

Prepare - Is there anything else? Write it down.

Notes to Self:

Prepare - Determine what you can give up or live without.

Negotiate the Salary You Deserve

Notes to Self:

Summarize your win, the result of the negotiation, to clarify your thinking.

Hardball rarely works.
You may win in the short term.
You might lose immediately.

THE TWO MOST COMMON QUESTIONS

There is no right or wrong answer to these questions. Your circumstances will dictate your course of action. I only offer a different perspective. Talk with male and female friends who are already in management to get their perspective.

WHO SHOULD BRING UP THE SALARY NUMBER?

One of the challenges in negotiation *She who speaks* is figuring out who should mention *first loses.* salary first. One of the oldest rules in negotiation is: "she who speaks first loses." I spoke first once and lost, and I learned a valuable lesson: salary can be used to qualify or disqualify a candidate. If your requirements are too high, they are likely to move your resume to the bottom of the pile. If they are too low, they might take it as an indicator of lack of performance or experience. They hold all of the cards. They know their budget.

When the hiring manager opens with "how much do you want?" without actually making an offer, I stop. It is tempting

Tip:
Always use a range for your salary figure. It suggests you're flexible and gives them flexibility.

to answer if you already have a number in mind. You want them to lay their cards on the table. You are better off sharing what you know and asking for their offer. For example: "I really like _____ about XYZ and want to work here. The salary for this position usually ranges from $A to $B. Your website outlines the benefits package. What is your offer?"

In that short paragraph I did several things. First, I revealed that I did my homework. Second, I asked them to clarify where we are in the process. Is he ready to hire me? Or is he gathering information to compare to other candidates? If they are ready to move forward, that is usually enough for them to reveal their information and the negotiation can start. At that point, if I like the basic offer but think there is more, I can follow up with, "Can we work together to craft a package that meets both of our requirements" or I can make a counter offer if I am prepared.

If they are not making an offer, then I'm in a tie with

other candidates. A firm salary number could disqualify me. I don't know the other candidates' compensation requirements. The negotiator may be looking to save money. By sharing my research, I give them an idea of my expectations without being specific. If they press for a number, "Can we work together…" indicates a willingness to negotiate and a desire to create a win for both sides. It also suggests there might be other things I would like or want more than hard cash. It allows the conversation to continue.

To the extent possible, don't be the one to bring up salary. Let them play their cards first. If you're in the position of responding to an offer, you stand a greater chance of crafting an offer that suits both of you.

SHOULD I PLAY HARDBALL?

Occasionally I will hear someone advise a woman to "play hardball." It is generally advice that is given when a woman is frustrated with a manager that she feels does not value her. She probably has one foot out the door but isn't quite ready to leave.

Hardball rarely works.
You may win in the short term, but lose in the long run.
You might lose immediately.

It is not a tactic I advise if you really want to keep your current working situation or land a new one. It generally backfires. Hardball isn't about how loud you can yell, pound your fist on a table or how firmly you can negotiate. It generally involves an ultimatum and unwillingness to compromise: Meet my conditions or I'm walking away.

The underlying assumption is that you have them over a barrel and they have to give in to your demands. That's generally not the case. None of us is so good that we're truly indispensable. Even if they accede to your demands, your power play will not be looked upon favorably when the time comes to make other tough decisions. One man I knew said "or else I quit" and his resignation was accepted right then.

I generally don't play hardball. Here's an example of a conversation with my supervisor where I was negotiating a promotion opportunity.

Let me start with a little background. Promotions tended to come when it was your "turn." I shouldered as much responsibility as the senior members of the group. I also knew the decision was not completely in my boss' hands. As part of a large department, he and his peers had to get together and duke it out for the limited number of promotions. I would be asking him to fight for me.

I asked my boss for an appointment. When we sat down to talk, I presented my case in terms of my responsibilities and the results I produced. I showed how my results were comparable to those of my peers and what was planned for the next year. It was a very positive conversation. He concurred. He was agreeable to supporting me for promotion. I felt good (dopamine and oxytocin). Then he asked, "What if I can't make it happen?"

It was a somber moment for both of us. I suddenly felt deflated. I sat quietly and then responded, "I really like working for you. It has been a great experience and I want it to continue. If the promotion doesn't happen then you will be looking for my replacement this time next year."

I didn't threaten. He didn't take my statement as a threat.

I didn't want to leave, but we both knew that might be my only option. We understood the company politics. I had paid for my mistakes but his peers had long memories. It would be a difficult fight.

Fortunately, I did get the promotion. Yet I was completely willing to let go of that job and the comfortable situation to go to a new place where my past contributions would be immediately rewarded with an increase in salary and position. You have to decide at what point you are willing to give up what you have to get what you want and feel you deserve.

Hopefully this last example gave you a good feel for how the process might work. I followed the same steps I outlined for you:

❖ Settle on the result.

❖ Prepare the case. Collect hard data about your performance.

❖ Prepare for the future. I had already decided what the next steps would be if the answer was "no." You need to do the same thing.

❖ Practice! I practiced my language in front of the mirror. I even practiced the deflating moment. I knew what it could feel like and how to manage my emotions to get through it. I also practiced walking away.

❖ Present professionally. I focused on the results I achieved.

❖ Respond to "no" professionally.

If you have done these things, you have done all you can.

It's easy:

Prepare
Practice
Present
Part ways

Wrap It Up

As I said in the introduction, I started out making less than a man who started shortly after I did. I didn't know to ask. Well, here's the rest of the story. He had one or two years of experience, went to a more prestigious university and he asked. From our hiring manager's perspective, he merited a slightly higher starting salary. At some point in our careers, he married. I didn't. While he worked as hard as I did, he was balancing family and work. Before the end of my time there, I had erased the gap.

When I interviewed for a position with another firm a few years later, I had more ammunition, experience and confidence. I knew to ask. As a result, I negotiated a bump in salary from what they were offering, a signing bonus, stock options and the amount of vacation I wanted. There was a little back and forth but not much. It was my dream job. I could have said yes to the initial offer, but I suspected I could get more and I did.

If you feel you are worth more than you are currently making, it is up to you to do something about it. You can't sit around, hope your supervisor will take notice and give you that promotion or raise. It is up to you to take charge. You have the keys to getting the salary you deserve. You understand how your gender and beliefs can undermine your efforts. You have a process for preparing for a negotiation and succeeding. Now all you need to do is go for your dream!

It's easy:

Prepare
Practice
Present
Part ways

THANK YOU

I hope you've enjoyed the first book in the *Career Strategies for Christian Women* series and you're armed with more answers to help you succeed in your career.

Please take a moment share a tweet #CS4CW about this book or follow us on Twitter — @CS4CW. I'd be very grateful. It will help others who are confused about how to negotiate a salary, raise, or promotion to find the answers they seek.

I'd also appreciate it very much if you could leave a short review of the book on Amazon. It will help me improve this and future books and help others like you decide if the Career Strategies books are right for them.

Many thanks!

Leslie

ABOUT THE AUTHOR

Leslie Knight is a human potential and implementation strategist and the author of the best-seller *Powerful Women: They're Not Men in Drag*. Her career has spanned 30+ years in various high tech roles, from systems programmer (bits and bytes nerd) to project manager, consultant and operations manager. She has worked for Fortune 50 organizations as well as smaller entrepreneurial firms specializing in leadership development and high performance teams.

This series of books was inspired by her two nieces who will be graduating in the near future. What do they need to know to succeed in their careers? It doesn't matter if you're 25 or 45, your faith is a part of your career. How can you be successful and let your light shine?

Please visit us at CS4CW.com.

Coming Soon
&
Appendicies

Appendix A: Cost of Living

If you would like to download a spreadsheet with calculations, please visit CS4CW.com/Resources. Decide now how much you want to save and do it! You can spend the rest. If you are relying on public transportation you might not have vehicle costs. Then again, you might have both. You might not have cable, but use services like Netflix and Hulu. Here are the typical expenses you need to consider:

Savings	Rent	Utilities such as
	Renter's Insurance	Cable
Car Payment		Electric
Auto Insurance	Health Insurance	Gas
Gasoline	Student Loans	Water
Public Transport		Internet
Parking	Groceries	Cell Phone
	Eating Out	Allowance
Total		

Negotiate the Salary You Deserve

Take the total and multiply by 12 to get your annual number. Now, multiply by 1.3. The reason for adding 30% to your total is to account for taxes (FICA, Medicare and income tax). You might need to allow for more. This is what you will need in salary to cover your projected expenses. Keep this in mind while negotiating.

Appendix B: Favorite Resources

Here are the books to which I referred or those which influenced my thoughts and writing. I hope you find them useful in answering your questions.

The Male Brain by Dr. Louann Brizendine. Dr. Brizendine looks at the impact of hormones on the male brain from birth through andropause (the male version of menopause).

The Female Brain by Dr. Louann Brizendine. In this book, she examines the impact of hormones on the female brain from birth through menopause.

7 Habits of Highly Effective People by Stephen Covey. These 7 lessons in personal growth are a must for any woman seeking to take charge of her life.

Leadership and the Sexes by Gurian and Annis. This is a great book for those wanting to improve their working relationship with the opposite sex. In addition to documenting some of the differences of the genders as leaders it lists a great deal of research that sheds light on some of our behaviors.

Shatter Your Speed Limits by Wendy Lipton-Dibner. This best-seller helps you examine your own limiting beliefs and break past them.

Powerful Women: They're Not Men in Drag by Leslie Knight. This best-seller consolidates a lot of the research from previous books. While it was written to men from a woman's perspective, many women have found it helpful in working with men and other women.

Appendix C: The IDidIt File

I discovered my need for a file to record my results and accomplishments when my manager asked for input to my annual review. How could he not know?! He's my boss. Well, I couldn't remember all that I had done over the course of the year either.

My solution is the IDidIt file, a paper or electronic journal.

On the first page, write down your job description and goals for the year. Write down the date. It keeps things in perspective.

Create an entry for each completed project or task as well as education you received, regular meetings you attend and reports you produce.

For tasks and projects, record:

❖ The date.
❖ The result you were expected to produce.
❖ The result you produced. What was the benefit to

the company? Everything you do should contribute to the company's bottom line by saving money, avoiding costs, increasing revenues or advancing their social or ecological goals.

❖ The challenges.

❖ What you learned. Did you gain new technical skills? Business perspective? Interpersonal skills? How did you grow from this project? How will the company benefit in the future?

❖ Any recognition or awards you receive.

If your goals and objectives change, write it down as well as the reason for the change. It's easy to forget by year end.

Please remember, this is not "Dear Diary." Avoid the temptation to talk about personalities and your feelings about them. Anything you write can and will be used against you if someone gets your file.

Keep it professional. Stick to the facts. If a silent movie of the project were shown, what would the viewer see?

Your manager is not omniscient. They don't see all you do and often they are unaware of the impact. Make it easy on yourself and keep a record.

Coming Soon

Additional books in the Career Strategies series will be released in 2015. Planned topics include:

❖ *Discover the Leader in You* – if you want to be in a leadership role, the time to start developing yourself is now.

❖ *The Truth about Working with Men* – conflict is inevitable, combat is optional. Learn the secret that will make working with them a joy.

❖ *Create Harmony in Work and Life* – addressing work/life balance from a Christian perspective.

If there is a topic you would like to address, please let us know. Send your email to: admin@CS4CW.com.

Stay tuned! More books will be coming soon. If you would like to be notified, please visit

CS4CW.com/Notify-Me.